FROM
NATION
TO
COLONY

Munroe Scott, a freelance playwright, biographer, filmwriter, novelist and columnist is a veteran observer of the Canadian scene. He was writer/director for the CBC-TV series *First Person Singular* (The Pearson memoirs), *One Canadian* (the Diefenbaker memoirs), and most of *The Tenth Decade* (the Diefenbaker-Pearson Years). He also wrote and directed two major CBC-TV documentaries on Mackenzie King and wrote the *Sound and Light Show* that has been running on Parliament Hill since 1984.

In March, 1987, he was presented with the Ontario Newspaper Association's Bell Canada Award for "Best Columnist, General Interest", for a weekly column entitled "Down Paradox Lane."

Books by Munroe Scott

Non-fiction:
   African Manhunt
   McClure: The China Years
   McClure: Years of Challenge

Fiction:
   Waltz for a Pagan Drum

Plays:
   McClure
   Wu-feng
   The Devil's Petition
   Shylock's Treasure

FROM
NATION
TO
COLONY

Free Trade and its setting
as seen
Down Paradox Lane

by
Munroe Scott

Tri-M Publishing

Canadian Cataloguing in Publication Data
Scott, Munroe, 1927 -
  From nation to colony; free trade and its setting
  as seen down paradox lane.

ISBN: 0-921050-02-X
1. Free trade and protection. 2. Canada-Commerce - United States. 3. United States - Commerce - Canada 4. Canada - Commercial treaties. 5. United States - Commercial treaties. 6. Canada - Commerce. I. Title

HF1766.S28   1988   382.9'71'073   C88-095284-9

Typeset: F.P. Comrie Production Ltd.
         Peterborough, Ont.

Printed: Hall Printing, Lindsay, Ont.

Published: Tri-M Publishing
           61 Hillside Drive
           Lindsay, Ontario, Canada
           K9V 1A3
           (705) 324-4946

Dedicated To My Grandchildren

Contents

Foreword

The Free Trade debate is the most important this country has faced since the election of 1911. The so-called "Free Trade" agreement sets us on a downward path that can only tie us closer to the American empire with a resultant loss of sovereignty. We are selling our souls for a mess of pottage. Munroe Scott's essays help make this clear.

I suggest the reader accept these mini-essays as what they are — passionately prejudiced. However, since the prejudice is for a humane, compassionate, egalitarian and evolving Canada that is greatly in peril, then the passion can only be applauded.

Pierre Berton
(Oct.6, 1988)

Preface

There have been more elegant subtitles than the one I have chosen for this book. The "Free Trade" reference is clear enough but I must explain that "Down Paradox Lane" is more than simply the universal address where we all live in these late years of the 20th Century.

For several years I've had the privilege of writing a column for an Ontario community newspaper, Lindsay THIS WEEK. The column is called, "Down Paradox Lane", and has dealt with everything from the inadvertant drinking of hummingbird nectar to handyman's woes to politics. The content has been limited only by the laws of libel and by my own freelance sense of decorum. To this day I have no idea as to the publisher's personal "politics" and consequently wish to thank him without in any way implicating him.

I began to realize some time ago that many of my readers were clipping certain columns and sending them to friends and relatives. Those readers have given me the courage to permit my views of Free Trade and its environment to be inflicted upon a wider audience. Without their encouragement, this small book would not exist.

Munroe Scott
Balsam Lake, Ont.

I

GET OUT OF IT!

(Sept.30, 1986)

We Canadians are on the brink of discovering the magic solution to all our problems. At the moment we're just grabbing at the edges of an idea but when it really sinks in, watch out.

I came to this conclusion recently while reading an in-depth article on the current thinking among some Ottawa mandarins, bureaucrats and high level politicians.

It's no secret that the government feels there are some farmers who should be assisted in getting off the land and that there are some crops that shouldn't be grown. But apparently what is really being advocated by some of our visionaries is that Canada should get out of agriculture.

CANADA SHOULD GET OUT OF AGRICULTURE.

It is not often these days that we are confronted with an idea of such magnificent scope; an idea that at one swoop ignores most of human experience and presents a startlingly fresh approach.

We Canadians have gone through a large chunk of this century telling ourselves that it's a good idea being reasonably self sufficient. We've brainwashed ourselves into thinking that we are rather blessed with resources — minerals, drinking water, hydro power, wood, oil — and that one of the greatest resources of all is farmland and people who know how to use it. Now, however, the time has evidently come to put away these childish illusions.

The brave new world we have created is no longer God-driven or even Nature-driven. It is Market-driven. This concept of everything being Market-driven is so beautifully simple that it's a wonder it's taken so long to sink into our skulls. When a human activity is Market-driven it either survives competitively or is abandoned.

Since there are others who grow fruit and vegetables more cheaply

1

than we do, and others who grow wheat (never mind what kind) more efficiently than we do, and others who can subsidize farming more heavily than we do, then it follows that Canada should get out of agriculture.

General Motors understands this philosophy. GM tells us that others can make vans more efficiently than we can and so it's about to help us get out of the van business.

We've been trying desperately for years to get out of the so-called cultural industries but narrow minded nationalists keep putting them on life support. It's time to pull the plug.

Many of our single-industry communities are in trouble and most of those are resource based. The market is not driving them anymore. Well, goodness, let's abandon those towns. Shut down the mines and close the paper mills.

Why in the name of heaven is Lindsay still soul searching about the fate of the Old Mill? It hasn't been water-driven for years and it's obviously not going to be Market-driven in the future. It's full of local history and symbolizes our settler roots, but so what? Knock it down.

Why is Fenelon Falls squabbling over maintaining a park-like access to a view of the gorge? There should be no problem. If that view isn't Market-driven then forget it. For that matter, how useful is the gorge except as a drain? Cover it over and build a shopping mall that sells things.

Never mind all the hassle about education. Add up the dollars and go for what makes the most economic sense. Our schools have been doing a lousy job of educating us anyway or else we'd long ago have realized that the human being is a simple, Market-driven animal. The schools have helped propagate nonsense about the quality of life and about man being an integral part of a God-driven environment. Well, I suppose the churches had something to do with that heresy.

And speaking of the churches, how are they doing these days? Is your church properly Market-driven? If not, to hell with it.

If Canada can get out of agriculture we can get out of anything.

Before I become too enthusiastic I must confess to having heard one comment that tends to dull the sparkle of the new philosophy. It was made by Jane Jacobs who recently received a Toronto Arts Award for a lifetime of achievement in urban vision. She referred to the planners who rely on statistics and mathematical analysis to plan the future. She called them "the bean counters" and said that the only problem with them is that they're nearly always wrong.

II

A FLAG FOR THE TIMES

(Aug.14, 1987)

I bought a Canadian flag last year. It was a modest size at a modest price and therefore comfortably inoffensive.

I raised my flag on the boathouse flagpole on July 1st. It made a brave sight as it unfurled and holidayers farther down the shoreline shouted cheerful approval.

The little flag flew nobly all last summer and it guided my sailboat home to a safe berth on many a windy weekend. Using it as a distant beacon I knew exactly where the water would become shallow, where the breakwater rocks jutted under the surface, where the gap led to calm waters, and whether the wind direction would permit me to enter that shelter or would force me to swing up to a deep-water mooring.

It wasn't until summer playtime was done that I noticed my little flag had been fraying along the outer edge. The outer bar was partially gone.

I had other things on my mind and I left the flag to fly by itself during the autumn weather.

When winter came the little flag still flew valiantly over the icebound shore. It was a useful weather vane. When I felt like cross country skiing a glance at the flag would tell whether a journey on the frozen lake would be treat or torture.

During the winter I noticed that the outer bar had been quite blown away and I vowed to take better care of my flag. Later, of course.

In March, I realized half the maple leaf was gone and I would have hauled it down then if the final blizzard hadn't struck.

By the beginning of last week there was no maple leaf at all and even the field of white was gone. All that remained was a tattered vertical bar of faded red about six inches wide. Not a flag at all; a mere nondescript pennant.

I took it down then, that poor tattered shrunken faded thing that had

4

once symbolized dominion from sea to sea and the aspirations of millions of independent people. It had marked my home and had defined my allegiance and I had ignored it.

I trudged to the house with the rag in my hand and went in and sat down and watched TV while the president of the United States made a stirring speech in the House of Commons.

He was in good form that day and he read his lines with the old skill and made the ridiculous sound plausible.

He proclaimed the seriousness of acid rain and made a sincere promise once again to think about doing something about it, thus continuing to ignore the most serious (next to nuclear incineration) long-term problem facing North America.

A goodly gaggle of our MPs applauded the president's fatuous promise of active non-action and my tattered flag, worn almost to the rope, took on new symbolism.

The leader of the most powerful nation in the world stood smilingly in our parliament and said his country would certainly talk with ours about Arctic sovereignty and Arctic defence and "other interests". The other interests presumably referred to oil rigs and supertankers and other Arctic commerce that can not only destroy our Inuit brothers but can also destroy global ecology. Our MPs applauded vigorously and I thought perhaps I'd re-fly my poor shredded pennant as a symbol of man's greed.

He talked with great passion and sincerity about free trade and its importance to our standard of living but he also threw in a linking comment about "open investment". By the time he'd finished talking about committing his resources to making this "visionary proposal" a reality there was a prolonged ovation from our MPs and my mind wandered history from the American Revolution to the War of 1812 to the Fenian Raids to President Teddy Roosevelt's aggressive cry of "Fifty-Four Forty or Fight". The Americans can't beat us, I said to myself while watching our obsequious MPs, but they can buy us.

The president threw recent history away and talked about the noble efforts to reduce nuclear armaments. He then threw logic away and described his Strategic Defence Initiative as a means of saving lives instead of targeting them. One voice cried out in protest but most MPs applauded this blatant presidential sophistry.

The voice cried out in anguished protest once again when the guest blamed all the horrors of Central America on the communists. The guest made light of the interruption and his parliamentary flunkies fawned to their feet to applaud aplomb. I would expect polite, respectful applause from Canada's MPs for an American president but standing ovations in a house devoted to debate, for a totally propagandistic speech immune from rebuttal, were immeasurably humiliating. I am thankful for the heckler who put bad-mannered honesty ahead of groveling mindlessness.

I'm going to buy another flag and I'll think of that heckler as I hoist it, and tend it.

III

OUR UNDEMOCRATIC CHAMPIONS

(Aug.25, 1987)

Why are the senators digging in their heels over the pharmaceutical bill? And for that matter why is the government being so granite-like in return?

I suspect the actions of both sides are closely related to what is being perceived as a major issue here in Ontario — good old Free Trade.

There is nothing new in our senators recommending major changes to a bill. And usually the government makes some adjustments because, dare I say it, very often the Commons decides the Senate is right!

So why all the froofurraw now? Why are both the government and the senators now suddenly becoming rock firm in their resolve to persevere with their own version of the drug bill? Why no legislative compromises?

Surely it's because the drug bill, with it's background of American lobby pressure and it's potential to create jobs for a few while increasing health costs for many, is a post Free Trade prototype. Consequently, in this drug skirmish, we're seeing the dress rehearsal for an eventual showdown between the Senate of Canada and the Mulroney government over Free Trade.

The last major conflict that had any similarity was in 1926 when Governor General Byng exercised his constitutional rights and Mackenzie King not only cried "foul" but turned it into a phoney issue that won him an election.

The senators know all about Lord Byng and what can happen when a crafty party leader begins to chant "democracy, democracy," as his battle cry. Right now they're making a few jabs and feints and have tried one body blow just to see what happens.

They're surely interested in two things, the least important of which

7

is how the government reacts. In the long run it's more important how we the people react.

Are we going to swallow Mulroney's hog wash about the undemocratic Senate interfering with the duly elected legislators? It's true that appointing senators instead of electing them is far from democratic, but it's rock solid constitutional. Or it was until the Meech Lake Accord when Mulroney agreed to pass the appointment powers on to the likes of Bill Vanderzalm.

Are we going to swallow the bilge voiced on the air recently by a senior staff member of the *Globe and Mail* who said the senators have "no moral right" to block the drug bill? Blocking legislation of which they disapprove is in their job specifications! What they have no moral right to do is to accept their appointment, take their money, and *not* do their job.

Lord Byng was following his job specifications in both spirit and letter when he refused to dissolve parliament for Mac King. What may well be looming on the horizon is the Senate invoking both spirit and letter to keep Mulroney from dissolving Canada.

The Senate can't block legislation forever but it can hold the bridge long enough for the electorate to get into the fray. Under our system, when a prime minister has the enormous and docile majority that Mulroney has he can do virtually anything he wants to do, subject only to the courts (undemocratically appointed, by the way) *and* the Senate.

We're coming to a moment in Canadian history when the anachronistic, undemocratic, pork barrel of a Senate is, for a brief moment, going to be the only champion we've got to face down a massively powerful and inept government that seriously believes that man does live by bread alone. The undemocratic Senate may be Canada's last democratic hope, and *that's* a paradox if ever there was one.

IV

(When the Free Trade negotiations were less than a week from the October 1st deadline, Canada's Simon Reisman suddenly broke off the talks.)

THE AGENT

(Sept.29, 1987)

My agent 'phoned the other day.

"Hi," he said, "just wanted to let you know I've broken off negotiations with the publishers."

"How come?"

"They wouldn't meet your bottom line."

"Well, if they're not interested ..."

"Oh, they're interested. To big city types your place looks pretty desirable."

"What's my house got to do with it? You're my *literary* agent!" I yelled. "My place isn't for sale!"

"You wanna show a profit or don't you? This is a money making proposition. Maybe I can work out a deal where they buy it but you can still live in it."

"I didn't retain you to do that!"

"Listen, there's money to be made."

"But it's not just me! What's my wife say? What do my sons think? What about the grandchildren?"

"Look. Everything's fast tracked for the end of the week."

"What's that mean?"

"It means if we don't deal by that time then they're picking up their marbles."

"I thought you'd already picked up ours."

"Sure," he said, sounding quite nonchalant, "that's the way you play this game."

I was becoming confused. "You were just supposed to be selling scripts," I protested. "You can't sell the house."

9

"Who's selling your house?"

"You just said so."

"No, no, no. You don't understand. In this game everybody lies through their teeth. That's how it's done. How else do you think we'd ever make a deal? Every time I come out of a meeting, your neighbours, and theirs, are all over the place. 'How'd it go? How much are you asking? What's their offer?' Naturally I'm going to lie to *everybody*! I wouldn't dream of selling your house."

"But you just said ..."

"Look, would I lie to you?"

"Yes, you just said ..."

"By the way," he went on, "I've let them have the copyright on those play scripts."

"Those were bargaining chips! — What'd you get for them?"

"Well," he laughed, "I guess you'd say I tossed them in sort of as good will gestures. To make them think you'd be an easy mark."

"Thank God the deal's broken off so I get those chips back."

"Oh, no. They're gone. They weren't within the framework of the deal. They were just PR."

I was beginning to choke into the 'phone. "You mean we've just *given* things away?"

"Look," he soothed, "you gotta understand. These guys are big business. They're worth dealing with."

"But my house!"

"Relax. Nobody's selling the house." There was a long pause. "Not unless they meet our bottom line."

"What kind of a line is a bottom line? Do you draw it, toe it, or shoot it!" I was beginning to rant.

"Easy does it, guy. Just have faith. You'll be on easy street."

"You said you'd broken off negotiations."

"Oh, that. Think about it. Their schedule says we have to deal by the end of the week. That puts pressure on us. So, okay, I break off now and we look hard to get. Suddenly that puts pressure on them. They'll make an offer, we'll make a counter offer, they'll counter that — you know — that's the way real estate deals are made."

"This isn't a real estate deal!"

"You know what I mean."

"I don't know what *anybody* means! That's the whole problem!"

"Gee, thanks." He sounded genuinely flattered. "It'd be pretty stupid negotiations if *everybody* knew what was really going on."

"Hold the 'phone!" I protested. "I'm not just anybody! And tell me — let's say your ploy works and they make the kind of offer you really want — like paying top dollar for the manuscripts *and* the house —"

"Now you're talking, guy!"

"My house isn't up for sale!" (I'm afraid I was yelling) "But if *everybody* has to lie on principle, maybe it *is* for sale! And if you sell it as my agent, then I'm stuck with a deal I never asked for — or else we're negotiating in bad faith!"

"Bad faith? Nonsense. This is business. But look, you're worrying for no reason. I know these guys. Believe me. I used to work for them."

"You did? As a literary agent?"

"Hell no. In real estate."

V

THE "EGREGIOUS" ERROR

(Oct.6, 1987)

In the midst of all the broohaha of Free Trade talks, postal strikes, and Blue Jay migrations, have you forgotten the Meech Lake Accord?

The Accord is now plodding its way into the Senate, and the provinces are supposed to debate it, but that's all a waste of time. No changes are to be allowed. The Prime Minister has said so.

Anyone who has ever signed a contract knew there could be no changes the minute the Quebec legislature ratified it. One does not alter so much as a comma in a signed contract without invalidating the original and returning it for re-endorsement.

Why are we going through the charade of being consulted? Why are we spending the time and the money and the nervous energy of passing this so-called Accord from committee to committee and legislature to legislature?

It is on the record that the only thing that can cause an alteration is an "egregious error".

Those of us who consulted our dictionaries to see what such an error might be, now know that it means a blunder of monumental proportions. It must be an error that can be classed as extraordinary, or remarkable, or enormous, or shocking. It must "tower above the flock".

In a 178 page report that is dripping with whitewash the Joint Committee of the Senate and the House of Commons finds no such towering bird.

In the Commons, the leaders of the opposition parties find several small birds but apparently see no high flying ones, for they agree to approve. I assume that if they did see the towering wings of error they would not, could not, approve though all Canada should sunder and the continent sink.

But deep in my soul I hear those heavy wings, and while reading the

12

well laundered report I was sure that others heard them, too.

I do not know whether the bird was ever named. It should be. But we are a people cursed with politeness and diffidence. We make tolerance a virtue to the point of being a sin. We shun honesty thinking it could be bigotry and in doing so become dishonourable.

The bird of folly I see poised high above future clouds is the vulture of racism.

I cannot convince myself that the new Accord is not about to entrench racism into Canada's constitution.

The culprit is the so-called "Distinct Society" section.

The politicians have gone to great lengths to describe that society without defining it. They have no need to. It means "French". While "French" can mean a beautiful language it is within human nature for that to sublimate into race. It matters not that pure races are vanishing from the face of the earth. It lies within human nature to substitute language, surnames, place of birth, and "culture" as surrogates for race.

Not only are we about to entrench a racist clause into our constitution but we are also entrenching a clause that makes it mandatory for future governments to maintain that racism!

Many women's organizations have opposed the distinct society clause partly because they can see the cradle being invoked as a tool to preserve race.

Aboriginal peoples are concerned because they feel their racial demands are made subordinate to the mandatory racial demands.

Ironically, neither women nor aboriginals seem to clamour for the overthrow of the original folly but instead, with monumental self-centredness, ask for constitutional protection from it.

We are told the Accord has finally reconciled English and French Canada.

We are also told that Canada as we know it cannot function without Quebec. But as I look back at history and ahead at the future I doubt that Canada can continue to evolve under the Accord.

This nation has been experiencing the unfolding of evolution but the Accord is about to impose the infolding of de-volution.

If Britain had entrenched a similar accord a thousand years ago would the isles not now contain a massive enclave of Saxons and, following the logic of fairness, ghettos of Normans, Angles, Picts, and Celts? Would not the splendid limbs of British common law and parliamentary democracy have been deformed in the womb?

Fortunately for us, Hadrian's Wall was always overrun.

Unfortunately for our descendants we no longer hear John Diefenbaker thundering, "I am not going to agree, whether it's popular or not, to erect a Berlin Wall around the province of Quebec".

Unfortunately for our descendants we are letting our representatives play as statesmen abroad, fulminating against apartheid, while they play politicians at home and entrench racism.

The egregious error is on the wing. Its talons are poised over our children's children.

VI

WOW, WHAT A SETTING!

(Oct.20, 1987)

I've got this great idea for a film musical. Totally fictitious, mind you, but there's sex, politics, violence — it should be a real dandy.

And wow, what a setting!

Think big. Think epic. I see this opus spreading itself all across Canada.

Your average epic tends to spread itself over a rambling period of time but the beauty of my idea is that the time frame is very compact. Everything is going on simultaneously.

Let me give you a sketch of the background action.

There's this big gathering of Commonwealth statesmen out on the west coast, see? They are debating uplifting, esoteric things like world bankruptcy, and other peoples' racial prejudice. Their verbal morality is very high and these dignitaries give a civilized tone to our epic. Think of them as a chorus of monks providing a background chant to counterpoint the foreground action.

In the meantime, while the Canadian head monk is reciting a sermon advocating international morality on a grand scale, his opponents in Ottawa are accusing him of selling Canada down the river to the United States.

Obviously, if his opponents are correct, then there is some pretty fancy footwork underway. Of course, nobody knows who is correct, because that's part of the fun of a good story.

In the meantime, Canadian newsmen, who can't figure out for themselves what is going on, are quoting an American newspaper tycoon as saying, "The momentous move toward uniting the two countries economically is very gratifying to me. For more than a decade my pop urged in his newspapers that Canada become a part of the United States."

Only those paying close attention to the dialogue will notice that the tycoon doesn't talk about uniting "economies" but about uniting "economically" which presumably means this new way is cheaper than doing it via a war, which has been tried in the past and didn't work, Canadians being irrational and stubborn.

In the meantime, off in a maritime province, a new government has just been elected and the electorate have goofed. They forgot to elect anyone from a second party. This introduces a certain element of comedy into the scenario and leaves the new and inexperienced premier with some interesting dilemmas.

But the premier's real problem is whether or not to be for or against donating Canada to foreigners.

In the meantime, national communications are being badly bent by a postal strike and the government, while its head monk is preaching motherhood on the west coast, is hell-bent on union busting. It uses scab labourers, cops and assassin-minded truck drivers, then brings in legislation that will fine people $1000 a day if they don't work. This has intriguing overtones of forced labour.

In the meantime, a chorus line of Ontario cabinet ministers are learning the choreography for a Free Trade soft-shoe-shuffle accompanied by entertaining lyrics. Their routine voices alarm over the possibility that Canada is about to be annexed to the Sates. With skilled buffoonery that would make Gilbert and Sullivan proud they promise to carry out a study that will make no recommendations and will not become the basis for any government action!

In the meantime, in Ottawa, a tiny group of dissenters from all three federal parties are firing SOS flares from the Peace Tower trying to tell us that Canada, as we know it, is about to be sunk by the Meech Lake Accord. The Opposition dissenters are particularly frustrated because their party leaders, while busily hauling up heavy artillery to shoot at Free Trade, are simultaneously snapping to attention and saluting the Accord. To change the metaphor, it's as though a ship's officers are repelling boarders at the bow while drilling holes in the stern.

What's that you say? All too bizarre? And it couldn't be going on simultaneously? Well, I suppose it is a little far fetched.

You see the politics but don't find any sex? Oh, come now. In this scenario just about everything is being raped — truth, nationalism, resources, the future, the past, unions, democracy, parliament — it's a gang bang from coast to coast.

Ah well, I suppose you're right. As a movie musical it will never fly. Too pornographic. How about an opera?

VII

THE QUEEN WORE BOOTS

(Nov.3, 1987)

All my adult life I have paid lip service to the idea that one major advantage of Canada's parliamentary monarchy over the American's republican system is that the former permits us to feel totally loyal to the head of state while being ferociously antagonistic (if we so choose) to the head of government.

There are other differences, of course, not all in our favour. But I have always felt sorry for those Americans who have had to revere the presidential office while they loathed the presidential action.

The secret, of course, is that our 20th century monarchs have kept themselves exquisitely removed from the political arena. Where public politics is concerned the Crown has kept itself in quarantine.

I was surprised when I first heard that the Queen, while in Quebec City, had endorsed the Meech Lake Accord. As the next few days wore on, and as I thought about it, my surprise turned to annoyance, then to anger, and finally to outrage. (A seventh generation Canadian Protestant of Scotch-Irish-English descent does not easily take umbrage at the Crown.)

The Meech Lake Accord might or might not be the greatest thing since God made His Covenant, but that's not the point.

The point is that it was reached by a highly questionable process smacking more of the behind-the-door wheeling and dealing of labour-management negotiations than of nation building.

Her Majesty said the wheeler-dealers showed a "strong sense of patriotism".

The eleven signatures approving the Accord were mere symbols until eleven legislatures should decide to adopt it and at the moment only two provinces had done so. Parliament itself had not yet voted and there were MPs who still had serious reservations about it (some said they would vote for it "holding their nose").

Her Majesty saw felicitous harmony and gave her blessing.

18

Some powerful national women's groups had been voicing deep concern over certain aspects of rights and freedoms they considered to be in jeopardy because of the Distinct Society portion of the Accord. Variations on their fears were being voiced by spokesmen for various First Nations. Quebec nationalists said Quebec was being turned into a ghetto.

Her Majesty proclaimed the Accord as a reinforcement of human rights and liberties.

Citizens of the Yukon and the Territories were in the process of pleading with the Senate of Canada to intervene in an Accord that is seen by many as dead-ending the north's political evolution. Not many people are affected at the moment but their territory is roughly the size of Europe.

Her Majesty saw an affirmation of unity through diversity.

That may be. That may not be. The point is that until the parliament and legislatures of this nation had made up their minds it was not, and is not, the function of the Crown to tell us what is or is not good for us.

The tender flower of unity blossoms with difficulty in a land as vast, as diverse, as harsh, as illogical as ours. In the past the throne, and the gracious lady who occupies it, has been one of the great intangibles that have watered the roots of unity.

In a single speech, Her Majesty, while applauding unity, tarnished the symbol of unity.

If she is in any doubt about the political nature of her words she has only to read the reports of Premier Bourassa's reaction. Bourassa, (who has such tunnel vision he looks at Free Trade by peering down a hydro corridor) was instantly crowing over the royal endorsement. That endorsement, he gloated, should ensure ratification by the provinces.

My heart sinks. In this country, which is far more free of spirit than it's leaders seem to think, royal endorsement might well be the catalyst required to unify and solidify republican sentiments.

What next? Will the Mulroney government, heartened by the royal error, coerce the Governor General into endorsing Free Trade? That should conclude the destruction of the brave, irrational, and inspiring experiment once known as the Dominion of Canada.

Her Majesty is human like the rest of us. Would we could all look back on careers as unblemished as hers. But she took a wrong step the other day — wearing boots.

VIII

SNAKE OIL?

(Nov.10, 1987)

Whoeeee! The lady likened them to snake oil salesmen. Yes indeed. Ms Margaret Atwood, Canada's internationally famous authoress, has said that the folk peddling the current Canada-Us Free Trade deal are pushing it like snake oil salesmen.

I've never met a snake oil salesman. Nor have I ever seen any snake oil. What is it, anyway? Is it venom? Surely not. That's mighty poisonous stuff.

Is it what's left if you boil a snake and throw away the carcass? Could be.

Salesmen who peddled snake oil were, I understand, pushing it as good for everything from hair restorer to an elixir of life. I can imagine them at the county fair, standing on the wagon tailgate: "Step right up ladies and gentlemen — good for boils, bites, and bellyaches — only ten cents a bottle, a bargain at half the price!"

Are these the charlatan's to whom Ms Atwood compares the pedlars of Free trade?

When I come across a sweeping generalization I like to test it by applying specifics (and I don't mean the herbal medicine being flogged from another wagon).

I applied this specific: If Free Trade salesmen are snake oil salesmen, does that mean our local MP is a snake oil salesman? Surely not!

For one thing, a snake oil salesman makes extravagant claims for his product without any proof to substantiate his claims.

Well now, a glance at *Lindsay THIS WEEK* last week showed that last week in *THIS WEEK* our man was eulogizing the economic merits of Free Trade and to prove his claim quoted both the Economic Council of Canada and the Ottawa Citizen. What more could one ask!

I understand that snake oil salesmen were notorious for offering absolutely no guarantees to back up their claims.

Our MP, to back up his claims, offered absolutely no — well, shucks,

20

we're too cautious in this paranoid society anyway.

A major problem with snake oil was that it carried no declaration of contents. It took the federal Food and Drug people to remedy that little oversight (and remedying it no doubt helped cause the demise of snake oil).

But it would be preposterous to think that our representative is pushing a Free Trade elixir upon us without knowing what it contains. Of course, you and I don't know what it contains. John Turner, Ed Broadbent, David Peterson, Bob White and the Parliament of Canada don't know what it contains. But our man must know what it contains otherwise he'd be just like a snake oil — oh, come now.

I suppose the biggest problem with snake oil salesmen was that they pushed their product as an answer to fantasies without ever suggesting (and often without even knowing) that its use caused unpleasant side effects that could range anywhere from loss of hair to eroded kidneys. The purchaser, in striving to improve the quality of life, could lose life.

Today's more canny customers are leery of modern snake oil. They expect the computerized drugstore to give them an instant print-out of any serious side effects. They go home and take a drug book off the shelves and read the fine print to see what witch's brew the doctor has ordered.

Surely our MP wouldn't advocate a potion while totally ignorant of the side effects? For instance, on energy he says we now have a secure market for exports. It must be a mere oversight that he doesn't happen to mention that we *must* export energy if called upon to do so; and that the deal goes beyond energy and includes resources. Nor does he happen to mention that it is still not at all clear whether or not water is included in the "resource" category. And that it seems the agreement isn't just about available resources but includes *reserves*.

Our man says that consumers should stand to benefit from more competition in "a whole host of personal services". He probably just forgot to mention that "personal services" include private health care companies. They're very big in the States. They're longing to invade the Canadian market but provinces like Ontario have fought tooth and nail to keep from developing a "two-tier" health system — meaning a good one for the rich and a sub standard one for the poor.

Is destruction of the one-tier public health care system a possible side effect of the Free Trade potion? The label doesn't say. Our MP doesn't say.

"Step right up, la-dees and gen-tuhl-men, get your snake oil here — no label, no list of ingredients, no warnings of side effects, no guarantees but the gen-u-ine ar-tic-le you may be sure!"

IX

LOYAL SHE REMAINS

(Nov.24, 1987)

I find it alarming to see the way the pro-Free Trade premiers and the prime minister are attempting to isolate Ontario as though it is some sort of latter day dog-in-the-manager. David Peterson is being forced to become the principal champion on one side of a conflict that is in a fair way of becoming Canada's civil war.

Some historians have lamented the fact that Canada has never had a revolution, but all major revolutions are preceded by civil war. We're now moving into that preliminary stage.

The real tragedy is that the pro-Free Trade troops appear to have no comprehension whatsoever of the concerns that haunt their opponents.

I have yet to meet anyone who is opposed to enhanced trade, improved trade, more trade, broader trade, even, I suppose, free trade. But I know a great many people who are not in favour of having less sovereignty and less control of their destiny. The problem does not lie with so-called free trade but with the Mulroney appendages of *Open Investment* and *Resource Sharing*.

Some of us are so dense we can't understand why, in order to do business with a neighbour, we have to give that neighbour an open option to buy our house, or to cart away our topsoil, or tap into our well.

Some of us are so addle brained we have the idea that when it comes to resources we, the people, are not simply exploiters but (strange concept) stewards. We have this bizarre notion that generations yet unborn will bless us or curse us, depending upon whether we conserve or destroy. We look at the system we are being asked to whole heartedly embrace and see a system that appears to be even more destructive than our own.

Some of us are so timid (or so our prime minister keeps telling us) that we hesitate to hitch our national wagon to an economy that is more and more totally devoted to building engines of war. We are so timid we are reluctant to endorse, without criticism, the dreams shared by a geriatric president and a one dimensional prime minister.

We like trade. We are traders to the core.

We also like Americans.

But some of us are so pro-American that we feel it would do them a disservice to abandon our dreams in favour of their realities. We have created a country that is, if not more generous to other people, at least more compassionate to its own. If, in order to be free to explore the paths of national compassion we say no to Open Investment, we are not being anti-American but merely pro-human.

The Americans have explored many frontiers, including Space, but we in our strange understated way have been exploring a social frontier. The result is a quasi-socialist-capitalist-republican-monarchical-colonial-independent-federal-unitary state that is quite unlike any other country on earth.

No one person or government made Canada. It is a product of history just as mankind is a product of evolution. No one person or government has any more right to abort this nation than Adam would have had to abort mankind.

What we timid folk fear is that one of the world's great national experiments is about to be terminated just as it is showing positive results in everything from race relations to health care. It is Machiavellian to distort these fears into bizarre statements that Ontario doesn't want Newfoundland, or the West, to prosper.

These notions of social evolution are difficult for politicians to put into words but I suspect that premiers Peterson, Pawley and Ghiz are more motivated by such strange notions than they are by the size of corporate profits. In this context, the attempt to cast Ontario's Peterson as a fat-cat oppressor of poor provinces is almost demonic.

I could be wrong in all my speculations. And Peterson, Pawley and Ghiz could be quite wrong in having reservations about the trade deal. Mulroney and Bourassa and Getty and Vanderzalm (and even Reagan) could be right. A Canada-US compact for Open Investment and unbridled Resource Exploitation might be the greatest social idea since man invented democracy. But if the timid souls who have doubts are denied the right to express their concerns in an election then the psyche of this nation will have been scarred forever.

It's ironic that such a risk is being run by a prime minister who came to power on a promise of non-confrontation, unity, and healing!

It will be a national tragedy if the same prime minister refuses to recognize the possibility that Ontario's motto, "Loyal she remains", just might refer to abstract loyalties that lie deeper than the pocket book.

X

FROM NATION TO COLONY

(Jan.5, 1988)

Some time ago I said that Canada is in the midst of a revolution. I see no reason to change my mind.

It is a revolution that is moving us firmly into a New Colonialism.

Centuries from now, historians will puzzle over the Canadian phenomenon. They will see the 20th century beginning with Canada a colony of Great Britain. They will see a brief sixty years (about 1930 to 1990) during which Canada emerged as a proudly independent nation. They will then see a swift decline into Canada as a colony of the United States.

It will have happened because of the naivete of Canadians who seem to be unaware of the facts of history, one of which is that empire follows trade.

The great empires of recent eras grew in response to trade. Britain, France, Holland — all sent warships and troops to support endangered mercantile investment.

The pattern was always relatively simple. Business moved in and established facilities and made investments that returned handsome dividends to the economy of the dominant country. When the locals got restless or other competition moved in, the dominant country reacted to the needs of its own business community and supported "trade" with might.

Often, the only way out of such colonial domination was via revolution. The American colonies revolted from Britain. The Indonesians revolted from the Dutch. The Vietnamese revolted from the French.

Canada was unusual. She moved to independence through evolution.

Canada is being unusual once again. She is *returning* to colonialism via revolution.

Paradoxically, the revolution is being conducted by a party already in power that is now inviting the world's most powerful nation to

26

consolidate the business entrenchments that inevitably precede the absorption into empire.

Future historians will be further amazed by the gullibility of Canadians who believe that the revolutionaries are "Conservatives" in the Canadian tradition. They are not. Their philosophy bears little resemblance to that of the nationalist party of John A.MacDonald and the populist party of John Diefenbaker.

The Mulroneyites are Neo-Conservatives, calling (under the guise of Free Trade) for Open Investment. Their slogan — "A Level Playing Field".

Open Investment entrenches empire and the Level Playing Field ensures its continuity. Once it's established, any change to that so-called Level Playing Field brings a reflex protective reaction from the controlling country.

Any nationalist movement that attempts to keep profits at home is a threat to a mercantile empire. It is no accident that the United States has consistently opposed *any* regime, anywhere, that impedes American business interests.

It is worth asking ourselves what the pattern of 20th century history would have been if the Mulronyites' Canada-US economic union had been instituted earlier.

Canada entered two World Wars almost three years ahead of the United States. Historians agree that Canada's contribution, both militarily and industrially, helped tip the balance. Could Canada have ventured so courageously if her economy had been integrated with that of the US? Of course not.

Canada moved as a free agent behind the scenes at the UN when the Suez crisis brought the world to the brink of another World War. The US was not even talking to Britain and France but fortunately independent Canada was trusted by the Europeans, the Americans, *and* the Afro-Asians. The result was a remarkable, and hopeful, experiment in middle power peace keeping. With an integrated economy Canada is about to abandon forever her right to a voice as an independent international moderate. That is a betrayal of global proportions (approved, paradox upon paradox, by the revolutionaries' Minister of External Affairs!).

With a totally integrated economy could Canada have remained clear of the Vietnam War? Her armed forces probably could have, but her peoples' labours and her resources would have been at the service of US policy.

Canadians are practical folk who see justification for some public ownership of utilities, for public health care with equal access, for regional subsidies — the list is long and most of it runs counter to the philosophies of the United States.

In the economic union of our new colonialism Canada will have lost her ability to sway in creative tension between the productivity of the right and the humanism of the left. She will be committed to the Neo-Conservative Right. Therein lies the revolution.

A people that is docilely willing to be stripped of such future options is a people devoid of both vision and honour.

XI

AN ELECTION INTERVIEW

(Jan.19, 1988)

A recent editorial in a Victoria County newspaper suggested that in the next election the prime minister should take great delight in referring to Turner and Broadbent as the Bobsey Twins, thanks to their apparent willingness to consider a coalition government.

I think this idea of giving free election advice to the PM is a good one so I've culled my memory to draw out the residual essence of the PM's actions, speeches and interviews. These I've put into one master interview that he can tape and have distributed via the Tory TV outlet to all freeloading newscasters.

The genius of this interview is that it makes very little reference to Free Trade, in keeping with the policy established during the '84 campaign, which of course didn't mention it at all.

Here we go. "Lights. Sound up. Camera. Action!"

QUESTION: Prime Minister, you once —
PRIME M.: Indeed, to the contrary. I promised to end patronage when there was no longer a living breathing Conservative to be appointed.
QUESTION: In the 1984 election debate you —
PRIME M.: One of the Bobsey Twins said he had no choice but to make certain patronage appointments and I said he could have said 'No'. You gentlemen of the press twisted that to mean that I should say 'No'.
QUESTION: Sir, how about —
PRIME M.: I can assure you the people of Canada are not going to stand by and let an appointed, undemocratic Senate block the will of the elected representatives. As for the possibility of an NDP-Liberal coalition I can assure you I will make full use of my patronage appointment powers to make certain that my undemocratic appointees will be in a position to obstruct any such coalition of elected representatives.

QUESTION: Your government —

PRIME M.: One of the Bobsey Twins wants to abolish the Senate. In a coalition will they abolish half of it?

QUESTION: Your government seems to have been in favour of —

PRIME M.: I say to you most sincerely that we are pro-Canadian. This is a great country, a strong country.

QUESTION: In '87, Canada Post —

PRIME M.: Eventually, by raising postal rates, by franchising to eliminate union wages, and by abolishing mail delivery altogether we will show that the service can pay its own way.

QUESTION: Some economists say that —

PRIME M.: Canada is vigorous and adventuresome. Have faith in Canada.

QUESTION: I beg your par —

PRIME M.: This has nothing whatsoever to do with South Africa. It is quite false to even mention the two in the same breath. Speaking with the same breath is for the Bobsey Twins.

QUESTION: May I ask, Prime Minister, how you intend to —

PRIME M.: Meech Lake was a great achievement in nation building. It may have given more power to the provinces but in a federation that is only their due. And just because all ten premiers and myself have to agree on any future constitutional change shouldn't worry anyone because this nation was built on consensus and compromise.

QUESTION: Speaking of consensus —

PRIME M.: It doesn't trouble me that Ontario, Manitoba and Prince Edward Island are opposed to Free Trade. Seven to three is unanimity enough. You can't run a country by committee and this has nothing whatsoever to do with South Africa.

QUESTION: Sorry, Prime Minister. What I was going to ask was —

PRIME M.: Believe me, when I say the Israelis used great restraint that doesn't mean I don't feel for the dead demonstrators. But instead of bullets the occupying troops could have used grenades, flame throwers or rockets, and it has nothing whatsoever to do with any statements made by the Department of External Affairs.

QUESTION: There seem to be conflicting —

PRIME M.: The Prime Minister speaks for the government of Canada and so it stands to reason that any contradictory statement made by one of his ministers cannot be government policy and was therefore not what was said at the time. I say, with respect, that the tape recorders always get it wrong. Except for the Bobsey Twins.

QUESTION: Tax reform has been a major —

PRIME M.: I'm glad you asked that. The new system has lowered all personal income taxes so that the major increases that have taken place since we came to power have been slightly reduced just prior to this election. The major sales tax impositions when they come after the election will be totally democratic — they will affect the rich buying luxuries just as they will affect the poor buying necessities. I say to you most sincerely, the status quo is no longer good enough for Canadians. Canada is strong. Have faith in Canada.

- - - - - -

Media people will notice that this interview has no beginning, middle, or end. It can be run as a loop, endlessly, to fit any time slot.

XII

THE GOD OF ALL

(Feb.16, 1988)

Yes, I listened to the Finance Minister's budget speech the other day. No, I am not intending to write about it.

There was, however, a constant refrain in his speech that set me to pondering one of the major paradoxes of our North American society.

It was more than a refrain. It was an invocation, a paean of praise, a mantra, a chant, an alleluia to *Growth*.

I've voiced some concern before with any system that feels our lives should be totally "market driven" and that judges all success by the profit shown on the bottom line. I've even worried that Profit had become a god.

How naive I've been.

Listening to the Minister of Finance I realized that Profit is merely a Tory saint.

The Great God of our entire society is not Profit, but Growth. We all worship at his shrine, be we Right, Left, Middle or Mixed.

We all sing alleluia to Growth. We feel buoyant and optimistic when the Great God Growth (GGG) is healthy. We wring our hands when the GGG is weak.

We have even named a devil as the antagonist to our deity. The devil's name is Stagnation.

We want the population to Grow so the market can Grow so demand can Grow so investment can Grow so productivity can Grow so the market can Grow, and the whole wheel of inter-related activities itself keeps Growing.

It's great, it's wonderful, and the GGG has indeed made his face to shine upon us.

We, the GGG's disciples, have a truly enviable standard of living. We, the GGG's faithful followers, live secure in the knowledge that if we worship faithfully and uncritically at the feet of our god, all will be well.

It's a marvelous religion. It's a shame that it can lead only to destruction.

Shucks, I don't mean moral or spiritual destruction but simply plain, old fashioned physical destruction. (Since the physical destruction meted out by the GGG will be visited not upon us but upon our descendants, I suppose there might be a little touch of spiritual damnation included with it, but think of that as a side order.)

Drive down to Big TO and visit Fort York. Stand in the middle of those few acres of ground with their modest fortifications and handful of barrack buildings and remind yourself that what you're seeing was, 200 years ago, just about *all* there was to Big TO. The 200 years have made quite a change. The GGG and his disciples have been some busy.

What wonders will be wrought in his name in the next 200 years?

We all know that the GGG loves to consume resources. Tiny voices in the wilderness keep reminding us that resources come to an end. But we, the GGG's devoted servants, have faith that our god's scientists will devise alternatives.

One resource for which there is no alternative is water.

Recently, I heard an interesting paper concerning the world's water resources. The writer spent some time discussing the problems in the States caused by the depletion of fresh water supplies. In virtually all cases the depletion could be traced to Growth, whether from sheer population pressure, or industrial use, or agricultural needs.

A truly chilling part of the presentation outlined various schemes that have been proposed, seriously but discreetly, for finding more fresh water, particularly for the American southwest. One grandiose scheme even pictures damming James Bay to make it a giant reservoir (more than half Canada's water flows north) and then diverting from that reservoir so the waters could be rerouted south.

A diverting thought indeed! What a libation. The waters from the northern half of a continent poured out at the feet of the Great God Growth.

And after the GGG has used it, destroyed it, depleted it, exhausted it, then what? Melt the polar ice cap? Yes, indeed. We who worship the GGG even see that as a possibility.

And after that?

Well, there'll be a brief time when we can admire the god's clay feet. After that, I guess, comes death and destruction. Oh, not for the planet. The dear old planet can outlast us. And not for us, personally, because we'll be long gone. But for our descendants. For mankind, womankind, babykind, all kinds.

In the months ahead we're going to hear eulogies to Growth from all political parties and I, for one, am going to have a great deal of difficulty with those paeans of praise. I won't be able to suppress the suspicion that the political high priests are all false prophets of a false religion.

XIII

THE LITERATI GAME

(April 19, 1988)

I played a frivolous game recently and attempted to analyze the words of one of our leading politicians.

By "analyze" I don't mean I tried to figure out what the man meant — that would be virtually impossible — but I attempted to figure out what his words told me about himself.

In this case the speaker was our Minister of International Trade. He was selling Free Trade. His words were quoted by the *Globe and Mail*, a staunch supporter of the government's continentalist philosophy, so I must accept the quote as accurate.

Mr. Crosbie is quoted as comparing opponents of the Canada-U.S. Free Trade deal to "CBC-type snivellers, the Toronto literati, the alarm spreaders (and) the encyclopedia-peddlers."

All right then, a word at a time, lets' see what this tells us about the speaker.

"CBC." The tone used here would be rather derisive and it instantly classifies the speaker as a post-World War II Conservative. (Diefenbaker also distrusted the CBC as being full of small "l" liberals and the current government has brought the dislike to an art form, all of which is curious because it was a Conservative government that established the CBC.)

"CBC-type." This must mean viewers, too, and not just CBC employees. One assumes the minister is thinking of all those folk who watch the *National* and the *Journal* and Hockey and *Man Alive* and reincarnations of Mackenzie King and who listen, faithfully, coast to coast, to *Morningside* with it's own special brand of CBC-type letter writers, reviewers, journalists, pundits, and generally interesting citizens. It's a courageous although foolhardy politician who assaults such a spectrum. Give the minister a star for guts.

"Snivellers." This is an interesting word. It tells me the minister is hard of hearing. Snivelling means "whining and weeping". The weeping

I can believe, but I suspect he's mistaking choking for whining. His government has been systematically strangling the CBC, bringing death gasps from what is virtually Canada's only national voice. The minister needs a hearing aid.

"Toronto." Since the speaker is not from Ontario the same derisive tone would be used here as with "CBC". The word "literati", however, adds a nice touch. According to the dictionary, literati refers to people of "learning" and "scholarship". The word "enlightened" is often used in the definition.

Since the minister uses literati in a derogatory fashion, I can only deduce that he is part of that old-fashioned class of Canadians who feared "men of letters". (I could never understand this because most of our Old World ancestors had deep respect for the literati. I've wondered if all that salt air and hardtack absorbed between decks in the old immigration sailing hulks eroded something from the Canadian ancestral brain. It's worth a Ph.D. study and I recommend some scholar put a lien on the minister's brain as a primary specimen for examination.)

The minister's derisive use of literati calls to mind another word he likes to use —"dinosaur". I used to think he was talking about opponents of Free Trade but now I wonder if it could be a mating call.

"Alarm-spreaders." This is truly revealing. Most nations honour their alarm-spreaders, from the geese who saved Rome through to the Americans' Paul Revere. The only people who don't like alarm-spreaders are invaders. Even the boy who cried wolf was, eventually, correct. I'll have to ponder this. Perhaps you should, too.

"Encyclopedia-peddlers." Time was when the sellers of encyclopedias tended to be youths working their way through college or too proud to go on the dole. Ah, well, times change. But what a curious portrait the words paint of a minister of the crown who implies that anyone selling volumes of collected knowledge must have a minuscule brain.

Good game, eh?

XIV

THE RETURN OF FARCE

(April 26, 1988)

The writers of low comedy should be on strike and all the rest of us should be on the picket lines supporting them.

The complaint? The politicians are stealing their material. Just as theatrical farce has started making a comeback the politicians begin doing routines that would make Moliere or Feydeau weep with envy.

The most obvious example is, fittingly enough, the current French farce. This involves fish poaching in Canadian waters by a boat with a name guaranteed to arouse the ghost of General DeGaulle, and, in Paris, much waving of the Tri-colour and wrapping of presidential candidates in the same.

The most farcical bit of dialogue in the script was the one uttered by the French senator who, having been given the overnight jail session that he went seeking, announced that Canada had a long way to go to become civilized. It was a masterly turn, carried out with a simulated sincerity that I like to think brought roars of appreciative laughter from coast to coast. The next routine should involve players popping in and out of doors all over France and it was a nice touch for Canada to send a non-elected cabinet minister to play straight man for the farceurs.

Those Canadian families who are still mourning the dead from two wars of liberation on French soil will of course be laughing the hardest.

The Fish Farce is in a league all by itself but the playbill has some other good listings. Take the Canadian environmentalist groups that are saying Mulroney should use Free Trade as a bargaining chip to get an acid rain agreement with the States. The Free Trade deal itself is Faustian — offering up a national soul in exchange for prosperity — but the environmentalists want to add guaranteed longevity to the deal, presumably so the loss of the soul can be mourned for a longer period. This would be serious drama but the wide-eyed way in which it's presented elevates it into the realm of good farce. Bravo, bravo!

There's another entry on the playbill and it should soon take over top billing. In Ottawa, the Liberal-dominated Senate has sent the Meech Lake Accord back to the Conservative-dominated Commons with some "improving" amendments. This will not only enrage the government but will discombobulate both Turner and Broadbent who have already voted in favour of the Accord.

The Accord already had enough farcical plotlines in it to spark an entire theatrical season but now the pace quickens. Watch for lots of pratfalls and mistaken identities with the characters all attempting to stand on the same spot without touching elbows.

In the meantime, even the Bi-lingual Illusionists are moving from magic to farce. Soon every major politician in the country will be engaged in attempting simultaneously to expand and restrict bi-lingualism. Students of theatre should find it fascinating. Political farce is going to have to introduce contortionists, the way opera pauses for interludes of ballet.

Even as I write this, the radio is droning on in another room and a reporter is announcing with a perfectly deadpan voice that all Canadian mail destined for Europe is to be shipped via truck to the States and flown from there to Europe via an American carrier. It is, apparently, a better deal. No comment is made as to whether it is a better *service*, just a better deal.

What new farce is this? Can we really get a better deal on a foreign carrier than we can on an airline we ourselves own? Woops, I forgot — we're going to sell that airline. Or are we? Aren't we going to sell it to ourselves? No, we're only going to sell 45% to ourselves, and we ourselves will keep possession of the other 55%. Our representatives promise not to use that 55% to dictate policy, so the control will not rest with all of us who own the airline but only with those of us who also own part of it.

The doors are flying open and closed, the actors are running, tripping, and mouthing inane absurdities. Stop! stop! My sides are hurting.

XV

A CANADIAN TRAGEDY

(May 3, 1988)

Wasn't it just last week I had come to the conclusion that the politicians were all becoming expert farceurs?

I take it all back.

Some of them are becoming rather good as tragedians.

I can't think of any other way to classify the attempted caucus coup in the federal Liberal Party than to call it tragedy. At any other time it would be mere drama or even, conceivably, comedy. But not now. Not this year. Not, for heaven's sake, the very day that Mulroney is standing in front of the American Congress saying he has the majority to pass the Free Trade bill and that he intends to use it!

That was an ominous statement. The prime minister didn't say he intended to call an election to get a mandate to give away control of our destiny. No. He has a majority and he intends to use it.

Whether the Free Trade Plus deal is Good or Bad or Indifferent it will leave this country psychologically fractured unless it is passed by a government with a mandate to do so. Only a unified opposition (with the help of the Senate) can battle the government to a position where it has to call that election in order to proceed.

But where are the troops of the official Opposition? Riding hell-for-leather to the pass? Rolling boulders into readiness on the heights? Digging elephant traps in the trail? No, no. They're squabbling like children over who should captain the team!

I search for an analogy and think of Leonidas and his Greeks attempting to hold the pass at Thermopylae in 480 BC. If they had fallen to bickering and squabbling over Leonidas' abilities the entire remaining history of western civilization would have been different. Even though they lost their battle they gave such a psychological boost to the rest of Greece that eventually the Persian hordes were repelled.

I'm not equating the total Americanization of Canada with being overrun by Xerxe's Persians. But I do think it's a major change of direction to move Canada suddenly and arbitrarily away from the evolutionary social course she has been following ever since Confederation. Such a move must not be made without, at the very least, a mandate from the electorate.

Did the Liberal Party not hear the prime minister making that promise to the American Congress? "My administration," he said, "has the majority to enact this agreement, and we shall." Those aren't the words of a politician intending to call an election first.

Does the Liberal Party think there will be an election before Free Trade Plus is passed unless the prime minister is battered into calling one?

The next few months are, metaphorically, Canada's pass of Thermopylae and just when the Liberal infantrymen are needed the most they try to mutiny!

General Broadbent and his platoon will no doubt stand firm on one flank and the ageing senators may well martyr themselves holding the other, but with the Liberal centre trying to assassinate its own leader the prospects don't look promising.

There is, of course, another way to look at the scenario. As Shakespeare's King Henry said before the battle of Agincourt, the fewer the men the greater the share of honour. When the time comes to stonewall the Free Trade Plus deal into an election, the NDP and the Senate may have to attempt to do it without the Official Opposition. The present Liberal MPs can then equate themselves with Shakespeare's "gentlemen in England now a-bed" who, said the King, "shall think themselves accursed they were not here, and hold their manhoods cheap while any speaks that fought with us".

A parliamentary confrontation of historic proportions should take place in the next few months and it looks as though the Liberals intend to stay home a-bed. So much for their once arrogant belief that they governed Canada virtually by divine right. In the country's hour of need they seem determined to prove their manhoods cheap.

XVI

A CALL TO COMBAT

(May 10, 1988)

With dissidents among the federal Liberals virtually committing treason by hamstringing their party just when it's needed the most, it's time to bring back the old idea of selecting individual champions to settle disputes by personal combat.

There's lots of precedent for this. Remember David and Goliath? And how about Hector and Achilles before the walls of Troy? And the tales of medieval Europe are full of encounters between heavily armed champions settling squabbles on the Field of Honour.

Doesn't the very phrase, "Field of Honour", have a better ring to it than, say, "Election '88"? And resurrecting the Field of Honour would make extraordinarily good TV.

I hasten to say I don't picture the champions using pistols, slings, swords, axes, maces, or even flails. Perish the thought. There are more civilized alternatives.

Some of our Scottish ancestors used to settle serious rivalries by rowing each other to death in fishing boats or, more creatively, by appointing champions to engage in name-calling contests.

I hereby recommend the re-instatement of the old Scottish name-calling contest as a mechanism for the settlement of major disputes. We could try it first on France (think of the global TV ratings), then domesticate it for the debate on Free Trade Plus.

Just a couple a weeks ago in this column I criticized John Crosbie, the Minister of International Trade, for name-calling and I do now repent me. It had not occurred to me that he was simply a modern-day practitioner of an ancient art form. But there we have it. The government has its champion already dressed and armed and he's been throwing down the gauntlet for months, only we didn't know it. So be it.

I have no desire to see the Free Trade Plus debate turn into civil war or any other similar indelicacy. But to see it settled with a champion lip to lip with the minister in a name-calling contest — well, now, that would at least make a grand final entry in the History-of-Canada book. (It would have to be printed verbatim in an appendix so future generations would know we didn't all just lie down.)

Choosing the people's champion shouldn't be difficult. Recently there was a letter to the editor of the *Globe and Mail* from a maritimer by the name of Michael. Michael had a few choice things to say about "the minnows, choughs, bunghole-corks, ideologues and kettle-menders who make up our federal cabinet".

I commend those few words to your attention. As an Upper Canadian I have no idea what most of them mean, but on the other hand I know *exactly* what they mean. We should consider Michael as a candidate.

Establishing the rules may be more difficult. Should the contest be multi-lingual? If so, would it be translatable? (One shudders to think what could be unleashed from our multi-lingual culture.) And can modern metaphor be used even though the minister might choose to fight on more traditional ground?

How would the judges compare the minister's "dinosaurs" and "literati" to a counter attack such as — "This net-working chip-wit, this bit-brained printout with the floppy disk tongue, this unfused surge bar, this mini-megabyte piece of silicone is trying to keyboard Canada into a permanent interface with Greed!"?

On reflection, though, and after another thoughtful look at Michael's letter, I feel we would do well to pin our hopes on the old tongue and, yes, on a maritimer. Michael writes, "The trade deal stinks like herring-guts in July, and it would take more than the slub-gubberly demagoguery of some gurry-tongued jackdaw from St.John's to make Canadians think otherwise."

It's been suggested to me that eloquent Michael is a ringer from Upper Canada. If he is, all I can say is, "God help the minister if a real maritimer takes up the challenge". Until then, I hope Michael is standing by. If we can opt for the Field of Honour and a name-calling contest instead of open rebellion, he's our man.

XVII

SANITY OVERHAUL

(June 14, 1988)

Until now I've made no comment about Canada's proposed submarine fleet but a recent statement on TV network news was too much to swallow.

The newscaster informed us that the nuclear powered submarines will permit Canadians to go "under the polar ice where no Canadian has ever gone before".

Canadians most certainly have been under the polar ice. Dr. Joe MacInnis and his gang were featured some time ago in full colour in the National Geographic with an under-ice habitat they had built. They were not only living under the polar ice they were shown walking on it, underneath, upside down!

The National Geographic has also chronicled Dr. Joe's search for the sunken vessel "Breadalbane" — a search that also culminated under the arctic ice. Of course, if the newsreader meant, "in *areas* where no Canadian has gone before," then fair enough. But who knows what's meant?

The subs are billed as hunter-attack craft, which has a fine macho ring to it. They were originally said to be required to uphold our end of our NATO commitments. Now they're being billed as intended to uphold our arctic sovereignty.

The fact that the subs represent the biggest single peacetime military expenditure ever made by Canada surely gives even a layman like me the right to scratch his head with some puzzlement.

These multi-billion dollar leviathans are, so I gather, intended to patrol the arctic passages and detect unauthorized intruders. They will be capable of shadowing such intruders and, if necessary, of taking appropriate action.

Surely a mere billion dollars or so, dropped into the hands of people like Joe MacInnis, could establish manned underwater research stations in strategically chosen places that would not only give us traffic reports but would also advance our knowledge of all underwater arctic systems! What better way to establish sovereignty than to populate the waters with researchers?

Granted, the inhabitants of a chain of under-ice monitoring and research stations would not be able to take action against unauthorized intruders — but what action are the subs to take?

Does cabinet actually picture one of our subs shooting, ramming, or otherwise sinking an intruder under the polar cap? — an intruder carrying, like our own subs, a nuclear power plant?

Have we forgotten the panic a few years ago when a Russian satellite carrying a tiny nuclear plant crashed in our north? (And it was already mostly burned up on re-entry.) Is cabinet actually contemplating a scenario in which Canadians would blow up a reactor, anybody's reactor, under the polar cap?

We are told the arctic ecology is not only the most fragile in the world but affects the biological environment of the entire world. Are we really intending to impoverish ourselves in order to have the capability of participating in global environmental destruction if our subs ever do what they're designed to do — hunt and attack?

A few billion in under-ice research stations and we could both monitor traffic and participate in global environmental *protection*.

I admit to being hampered by memories of World War Two when it would have been a fatal handicap to have had to rely upon France, or even Britain, for our major armament. I suppose, however, that any modern confrontation will be over so fast that the question of parts and replacements will be irrelevant. But I can't escape the nagging thought that a multi-multi-billion dollar sub fleet is equally irrelevant.

Ottawa seems to be operating at such great levels of irrationality these days that I am moved to question my own sanity. The sub program will impoverish us and risk ecological destruction in order to protect sovereignty. The Free Trade program will give away sovereignty so we won't be impoverished. I think I'll find a clinic and check the old brain in for an overhaul.

XVIII

UNDERSTANDING ECONOMISTS

(June 21, 1988)

It's a magic time we're living in, in which a Big TO parking lot gets transformed into gardens and numerous politicians get transformed not only into statesmen but into economists!

I've never really known what an economist is. I know Diefenbaker used to say that if a PM wanted ten different opinions all he had to do was consult ten economists. I take it economists must at least be free thinkers.

I own a renegade Webster's dictionary that defines an economist as a person who knows more about money than the man who has it. The same gem of a reference book struggles with defining "economics" and finally, overcome with honesty, opines that it's the way things would work out if we only let them. It also says economics is the art of stating the obvious in terms of the incomprehensible.

A good mix of politics always helps to obfuscate the obscure and I expect the incomprehensible quotient for Canadians should continue to rise long after the Economic Summit is over. After all, we do have a major Free Trade Plus debate coming up and there must be a federal election somewhere on the horizon.

The period leading up to an election is a good time for the layman to study economics. The government (any government) tries to use economics as a magic wand to prepare the way for a triumphant return through the portals of power. One of the most amazingly blatant uses of the wand occurred a few years ago when the Trudeau Liberals waved it over the election cauldron and suddenly produced a gift of harbourfront acreage for Toronto.

The wand is waving again, on an almost daily schedule, as the Mulroney Conservatives announce program after program, all involving large amounts of money and all to be implemented over a number of years (provided, of course, that they are re-elected).

It's in these pre-election times that we are privileged to learn what our governors think of economics, and of us.

An illuminating description was given almost half a century ago by a Chinese scholar, Lin Yutang, who was working in the States.

"Economics," he wrote, "makes no difference between human mouths and pig's snouts, and all the charts and dissertations on food and populations and tariffs are no more than the counting of snouts. The idea is that if you segregate the hogs in different sites and throw in enough hog fodder, with the fences neither too high nor too low between them, the hogs are going to live in peace, and then a millennium will descend upon the earth."

He named his theory, "swine-and-slops economics".

It's a fine name and an intriguing theory. I intend to use it during the next few months as a touchstone to test the quality of all economic pronouncements.

I've already been eyeing the programs dealing with day care, family violence, AIDS research, french translation in Saskatchewan, billion dollar development projects in Quebec, etc., etc., to see whether they are substance or slops; to see whether we are viewed as people or hogs. So far, hogs are winning hooves down.

It's particularly enlightening to try the swine-and-slops touchstone on the Free Trade Plus deal. Virtually every argument put forth in support of the deal has to do with promises of improved income and cheaper goods. Every time the Free Trade salesmen open their mouths I hear the slops landing in the trough.

A few weeks ago I watched TV in horrified fascination as an economist with the Howe Institute said, "It hasn't worked". The context was such that I could only interpret this to mean that he thought *Canada* hasn't worked! Canada can be mightily improved in many ways but if it hasn't worked I don't know any country that has.

I couldn't understand where this economist was coming from, or going to. Until I tried the "swine-and-slops" test. Then his economics fit right into place.

XIX

DISGRACING THE AIRWAVES

(June 28, 1988)

As I write this it is Wednesday morning, the 22nd of June, almost a week before you will be reading it. By then, you will know what I don't know now, which is whether anyone else is feeling as steamed up this morning as I am over as blatant a bit of propaganda as ever disgraced the CBC airwaves.

I am not referring to the coverage of the Economic Summit. That simply reminded me of a Hollywood benefit for an oldtimer. The only thing I can't understand about that is what the two thousand journalists were doing besides eating and drinking. (They couldn't even count — estimates of their own numbers kept oscillating from two to four thousand!)

Even Mulroney's proud flaunting of the Free Trade "endorsement" was acceptable. In spite of the wording of the statement we know that one of the leaders, Takeshita of Japan, has severe reservations. What was more revealing was that Mulroney obviously considers that the views (even partially contrived) of six foreign politicians should carry more weight that the views of five million Ontarians and their premier, the only politician in the world (as far as I know) holding power with a mandate concerning Free Trade.

But none of the above even rumpled my equanimity. It was CBC's *Journal* that got to me.

Did you see the segment (June 21st) with the economists predicting what the world will be like 20 years from now?

If you did, you must have been fascinated by the cheerful way they forecast the existence of European, North American, and Japanese-centered trading blocs, each of them a mighty economic union and inter-reacting with each other in a global economic machine.

They saw GNP rising, interest rates dropping, standards of living escalating, and free enterprise flourishing as never before, all of it market-driven.

I was mesmerized. They talked with wide-eyed anticipation, like small boys imagining a castle in a forest. With the same guileless manner they cheerfully admitted that the have-nots would still be have-nots. South America might not participate, "except possibly for Brazil", and they admitted that no-one might "want" Africa. (Except, I suppose, as a dump for toxic waste.)

They never considered the question of our own have-nots, but gave the impression that we in the blocs, 5000 years of experience to the contrary, would all be affluent.

These fellows waxed even more enthusiastically eloquent when they fell to discussing the social dynamism of international corporations. At this point I exclaimed in horror, "These guys are extolling the death of democracy!"

Barbara Frum was inexplicably and lamentably acting as a straight woman for these starry eyed one dimensional simpletons but at this point she, too, interjected a protest. She was told, however, that the whole process was going to increase "democratization".

It seemed, however, that what they meant by democratization was that there would be an enormous number of small companies flourishing and that they would "take power away" from the multi-nationals. Unless my ears had turned backwards on my head, I was listening to men who were looking forward to government of the companies, by the companies, for the companies! All of which was to guarantee affluent happiness for we the people.

I thought I must be hallucinating as they went on to forecast a constant decrease in the need for government intervention. They didn't use the term "withering" but they drew a picture of the withering away of government.

Shades of Karl Marx and the communist dream! The withering away of government has always been *the* central fallacy of "pure" communism. And here, at the end of Summit '88, the CBC was giving an uncontested national platform to "experts" preaching the same fallacy in the name of free enterprise and Free Trade! There was no challenge, no rebuttal — it was dangerous and blatant partisan propaganda.

If, by the time you read this, the *Journal* has aired balancing opinions, then I apologize. If not, I accuse.

XX

A PATRIOTIC CONVERSATION

(July 5, 1988)

It was Canada Day and I was reading in my study when I heard a rustle from beneath a newspaper I had carelessly tossed to one side. I lifted one corner and there was my old friend.*

"Newshawk," I said, "why are you sitting all huddled up like that? And why are you whimpering?"

"I'm cracking up! I'm paying too much attention."

"Attention to what?"

"The words," he whimpered, "the words." He glanced around furtively, then whispered. "Do you ever listen to the words?"

"I try to. When people talk."

"Yes, but when they sing?"

"Oh, oh. You've been singing 'O Canada'?"

"I thought it would be safe," he blubbered. "Once a year, anyway. But then I started to pay attention —" his eyes lost their focus for a moment then, with an effort, he pulled himself together.

"Glorious and free," he quoted. "What's it mean?"

"Glorious," said I, pompously, "means possessing exalted renown. You know, illustrious fame."

"Oh sure," he said, "but I looked it up. It also means hilarious from drink!"

"Well — take your choice."

"I tried to." He looked furtively around, then lowered his voice. "The exalted version doesn't fit."

I protested. "We can't sing, 'O Canada, plastered and free'!"

"But that's just it," he said, pulling the paper over his head, "if we're not plastered how can we believe the 'free'?" There was a long pause. "You see, I looked 'free' up, too. It means subject neither to foreign

* This old friend makes random visits to Paradox Lane. He is a would-be journalist but defies more accurate description and definition.

49

domination or to high-handed government."

"My poor old friend. Pay more attention to the music. Think of the words as a vehicle for the notes. Enjoy the sound, the occasion, the togetherness, the —"

"'We stand on guard for thee,'" he said. "I thought the country is supposed to stand on guard for us?"

"Sure. That, too."

"But which comes first? And if Canada commits suicide for us, then what do we stand on guard for?"

"You're right, old friend, you are coming unstuck."

His eyes filled with tears and he scuttled under a chair. "Can't help it. Been listening to the words." His voice was muffled but I could still hear him. He began to sing! "'True patriot love in all they sons command.'"

"That's better," I said.

He broke off. "No, that's worse. What is it? A hymn or a prayer? Why 'command'? Are we asking to be *ordered* to have true patriot love? If we don't have it naturally how can it be commanded? And is there a false patriot love?"

"I expect so."

"How do we know a true one? And what's patriot mean?"

"Oh, come now," I protested, "a patriot is one who stands up for his country."

Newshawk emerged from hiding and almost stamped on my foot. "You see?" he said, angrily, "you don't know, either. 'Way back in 1837 and '38, all those rebels — some marching on Toronto — some encouraging Americans to invade us — they're in the history books as *patriots*! And they lost! If the patriots lost, who won? When we pray for true patriot love are we exhorting ourselves to march on the government?"

"Ah, ha, old friend, you've hit on it. Yes indeed. Don't mistake government for country. True patriot love demands that every so often we march on Toronto, and Quebec, and Victoria, and oh yes indeed, frequently on Ottawa."

He brightened. "Glorious patriots?"

"You bet. Delightfully looped rebels. That should be us. Cling to that

50

thought when you sing 'O Canada'. In the meantime, my friend, try to enjoy the music."

XXI

A MIDSUMMER'S TALE

(July 19, 1988)

Once upon a time there was a Prime Minister who was fearfully afraid of calling an election for fear the people would rise up in their wrath and smite him with both ballots and boxes. Bursting with an amplitude of apprehension he showered promissory notes upon the people.

He had painted himself into the proverbial corner by making a Munich-like treaty with a powerful and aggressive neighbour. "There will be trade in our time," said the Prime Minister, while inwardly quaking with the knowledge that his time could end with the inevitable next election if that election were to be fought on the basis of a treaty for which there was no precedent, no mandate and no need.

And then a delightfully devious thought struck him and he prayed mightily that his treaty would be opposed by the venerable members of the august Senate. "We will march to victory at the polls," he thought, "by claiming that the will of the peoples' representatives is being thwarted by the non-elected members of a party-dominated Senate."

It was, indeed, a happy thought, and the time came when the non-elected senators, carefully considering their constitutional duties, had no choice but to oppose the Prime Minister and his guileful treaty. And the Prime Minister and his henchmen smote the senators with mighty (and often delightful) rhetorical accusations of being undemocratic, unelected, and non-responsible.

And it came to pass that the Prime Minister, accompanied by his well-trained and obedient cohorts, marched in a great election parade. They were clothed in costumes representing the armour of democracy and drove before them actors in chains representing the nasty tyrants of the undemocratic Senate.

But while the bands played and the flags waved and the promissory notes filled the air a studious youth on the sidelines studied the Constitution and, for all to hear, announced: "The Senate is written here, in all it's strangeness, but the Prime Minister doesn't exist!"

Others heard him and took up the cry and, as people were wont to do in those days, they all studied the Constitution. And lo and behold the youth was right! There was much detail in both large and small print about the senators but there was nary a word, syllable, or even breath about a prime minister.

There were words about a Privy Council to give "advice" or even "consent" to the ruler but no words suggesting that the council itself could rule. Studious youths, turning in frustration to the encyclopedia, discovered that a political entity called a "cabinet" had become the only active part of the Privy Council. Looking at the reality and the parade the same youths deduced that the cabinet had taken upon itself powers far beyond those of either advice or consent. And the Prime Minister had taken unto himself the cabinet.

Further search of the Constitution could find no mention of political parties, not even the one that was the prime participant in the parade. Whereupon a youth who was much addicted to statistics announced loudly that the Prime Minister had been elected leader of his party by a mere majority of 269 votes!

"No," cried the Prime Minister, in alarm. "I was elected by the people!"

The youths found this to be true. He was indeed elected to Parliament, as a simple member, by a total of 28,208 people!

Amazed, the people pondered the Prime Minister's power and the way he controlled government and dictated rules and made international treaties altering the national destiny. They began to listen carefully to his rhetoric about democracy and they recalled that, according to the Bible, the jawbone of an ass could be dangerous.

And it came to pass that there was a great cry calling for the curbing of undemocratic prime ministerial powers, and the Prime Minister and his cohorts were harried from the parade.

A new Prime Minister curbed his own powers, the Senate voted itself into reform, and everyone lived happily forever.

(The day after this column appeared, Mr. Turner announced that the Senate would block the Free Trade Bill until after an election, thus bringing to pass the first part of the fairytale.)

XXII

(Friendly) LETTER TO THE PM

(Aug.2, 1988)

Dear Prime Minister;

Please call an election soon and, preferably, make it a short one. If you don't, we're all going to be done in by the word "undemocratic".

I know that you reap a lot of joy out of accusing Mr.Turner and the senators of being undemocratic. But what if people start asking "What *is* democratic?"

What happens then?

We Canadians are raised from the cradle being told that Sir John A. MacDonald considered that the Senate's prime function should be to provide sober second thought. If the Senate now decides that *all* of us should take a sober second thought, is that not superbly democratic?

I must confess I have difficulty knowing what "democratic" means. I've been watching you to see if I can get some clues. I noticed some time ago that you and the ten premiers met behind closed doors for an all night bargaining session and came up with an agreement that in effect alters the Canadian constitution. Your government told Parliament that agreement was non-negotiable. Was that democratic?

We are taught in school that one of the great democratic achievements of our forefathers was the winning of "responsible government". I guess a lot of us think it means government is responsible to the people but you know and I know that what it meant at the time was that the executive, namely you and your cabinet, should be responsible to the House of Commons. I get the impression that nowadays the majority in the House is subservient to the prime minister. Is that democratic?

I notice that your government is following the traditional pre-election strategy of bribing voters with their own money, something the opposition parties can't do. Is that democratic?

Someone once said that democracy is the suspicion that more than half the people are right more than half the time. It occurs to me that in the next election more than half the people may decide that your government should be given retirement but since their votes will be split between two parties you'll remain master. Is that democratic?

I admit that you are already in an unfortunate and unenviable position as a result of the gross but accidental majority conferred upon you by an electorate that was fed up with your predecessor. Abraham Lincoln explained your problem rather well — "As I would not be a slave, so I would not be a master... Whatever differs from this, to the extent of the difference, is no democracy."

Your heart must ache as you relentlessly follow your path of radically altering the nature of our country by exerting the powers of master. But an election would help. It would give the people the opportunity to relieve you, if they so wish, of the enormous burden of being (according to Lincoln) undemocratic.

If you continue to shout "undemocratic" from the rooftops I'm really worried that people will start looking at the way our appointed judges are able to overrule laws made by Parliament. Is that democratic?

Perhaps you should have been turning your formidable power toward democratising our system instead of rebuilding the country in your own image. Of course, true democratization would lessen that same power so you're in a catch 22 position.

As an educated man you probably know that Thomas Carlyle warned over a hundred years ago that democracy, by it's very nature, is "a self-cancelling business". It's a warning that must give sleepless nights to a democratic prime minister.

Anyway, take heart. Remember that Plato called democracy a charming sort of government, full of variety and disorder, dispensing equality to unequals.

There seems to be some disorder on the horizon but, for all our sakes, please soft pedal the "undemocratic" chant. You might accidentally start us all thinking and the whole house of cards will tumble down, with you on the bottom of the heap.

XXIII

"X" MEANS "MANDATE"

(Aug.23, 1988)

I've just had a great idea! It came along when I was on the verge of apoplexy brought on by the word, "mandate" — the thing the Mulroney government claims it has and that the opposition claims the government doesn't have.

Do the Multories have a mandate to govern? Sure. I guess so. They must have.

But what does "govern" mean? Ah, there's the rub. Surely it at least means to function within some set rules, one of which is not to give away the store just because you've been told to manage it.

I've been doing some personal soul searching on this because I certainly gave my vote to our Tory MP in the '84 election. But by golly, Free Trade Plus was not in his job specifications at that time and I refuse to agree that I mandated any such thing. (Since I consider the mandate I did give is being abused I intend to cancel it at the first opportunity.)

I'll get around to the great idea in a minute but to balance the scales of apoplexy let me just say that the New Democrats are upping my blood pressure these days, too. Just a few months ago I had myself convinced they were a reasonable alternative to the Multories. (I pictured the NDP as a good mahout for the economic elephant!)

Trouble was, I'd been ignoring their long standing desire to abolish the Senate. Not just to reform — to abolish. And they're not relenting one little bit.

If there is one thing for which we should be eternally grateful to the Mulroney government, it's for rubbing our noses in the dangers of our system.

We've let a system evolve in which a strong minded PM with a suitably subservient cabinet and a healthy majority in the Commons can literally do anything he wants, including using millions of the taxpayers' dollars to tell the same taxpayers that locking the country into a more ruthless economic system is for their own good.

With the Multories herding us into ultimate economic union with the United States it's sobering to realize that without the Senate it would now be game over for Canada as we know it.

It may still be, but if the Senate holds firm at least a genuine mandate for national capitulation will have come from the electorate. Obviously, we need the Senate for our self respect.

But if we *do* abolish or neuter the Senate (and given another five year majority there's no telling what the Multories might do), then I have an idea.

Let's change the electoral system so the party with the most votes doesn't form the government but forms the opposition! Then the only mandate that I as a voter can be considered to have given is a mandate to ensure good government by electing a good watchdog.

Given this system the only government that could wield majority power would be a coalition of the losers. Coalitions, by their very nature, don't lend themselves to single minded control.

I can see this system putting an end to patronage and election bribery. What's the point of a government buying the electorate's affection if, when it's got it, the inevitable result will be to put itself into the opposition?

Optimists deny that elections are won on negatives more than on positives. But anyone with a long memory knows that the governments of St.Laurent, Diefenbaker, and Trudeau eventually foundered on voter antipathy.

Voting *for* the opposition would at least let us exercise our vote in a positive frame of mind. Wouldn't that be nice?

This is an idea the NDP should run with. Making the majority party form the opposition should be a platform plank right alongside the one for abolishing the Senate. The first makes the second practical.

In the meantime, since I believe in the watchdog function of the Senate, and since I'm fond of Canada, imperfect though it is, I see myself returning to the Liberal ballot box, just as in the early days of Pearson and of Trudeau. Paradoxically, these may be the latter days of Turner but since the "X" means "mandate" I see no alternative.

XXIV

THANKS, BUT NO THANKS

(Sept.13, 1988)

An envelope came along the other day. It contained two clippings from *The Financial Post* dealing with the Free Trade deal. One, an editorial, was headed, "Hardly a sellout". The other, a byline article, was headed, "Free trade critics haven't read treaty, or GATT".

There was also an unsigned, handwritten note saying, "There are none so blind as those that will not see".

Naturally, being an insecure type, I assumed that my anonymous correspondent was telling me that I'm blind in my pig headed opposition to the Multory Free Trade Plus deal.

I have read the clippings and agree with some of their basic points. There's no doubt that most of us, myself and John Crosbie included, have not read the entire Free Trade document. But as one article pointed out, even Mr.Crosbie's deputy minister "keeps a dog-eared copy of GATT in his briefcase — not because he has a bad memory but because it is that kind of a legal document".

"That kind of a legal document" is not, I fear, for the likes of me, and short of going to law school I don't know what to do about it. I don't suppose my member of parliament has read it either, and it would be uncharitable to ask.

An interesting position taken in both articles was that the trade deal is "a balanced and reciprocal agreement". Point well taken. What the US can do to us we can do to them. The mouse can buy the elephant and the elephant can buy the mouse. They can share our resources and we can share theirs.

It is, I suppose, a mere detail that we happen to be the ones sitting on the minerals and waters of the Canadian Shield, and the oil of Hibernia, and the tar sands of Alberta, and the potential of the Arctic.

In a balanced and reciprocal agreement it is hardly worth mentioning that we're the ones with hydro-electric power coming out of our ears

58

but one does wonder what the balancing factor could be. I suppose it's that we get to sell it to ourselves at whatever price the elephant is willing to pay, in spite of the fact that in a vast, cold, northern country we need cheap energy to keep us warm, mobile and competitive.

The more I read the clippings sent by my anonymous correspondent the more I find myself wondering if the cryptic note was perhaps suggesting that the authors of the *Financial Post* items are blind?

But the fact remains that we, the voters, don't read these massive documents and most of us wouldn't understand them if we did. We approach these issues guided by intuition, instinct, prejudice, experience, and gut reactions. It may seem a poor way to run a ship but in the final analysis there may be more insight in intuition than in legalese.

What it really comes down to is that when we're baffled by the merchandize we assess the salesmen.

I see a principal salesman who opposed Free Trade while applying for office and then went for it the minute he was in; who opposed patronage to get elected and then became a practitioner par excellence; who preaches national unity while building racism into the constitution; who advocates a market-driven economy while cynically pouring pre-election money into vast oil projects that may never be commercially viable; who preaches national independence while bootlicking an American president most Canadians wouldn't have elected dog catcher.

I see an assistant salesman who is supposed to have a fine mind and an excellent education but who appears to have a vile tongue and a mean spirit; who, as the scion of a wealthy Newfoundland family, comes from a merchant tradition not noted for uplifting the poor; who was raised by a father vociferous in opposing Newfoundland's federation with Canada and in favour of joining the States.

I may indeed be blind in assessing the merchandize but I don't need a law degree to assess the salesmen. I must react intuitively the same way any of my canny ancestors would have done and say, 'Thanks, but no thanks'.

XXV

CRIME OR TRAGEDY?

(Sept.30 for Oct.4, 1988)

It is early Friday morning as I write this and several important questions are still unanswered.

Will the prime minister choose today to announce an election?

What can Ben Johnson say that hasn't already been said for him, against him, or about him?

Does the last Angus Reid poll that shows the Multories enjoying 40 percent popularity indicate that Lin Yutang's "swine and slops" theory of economics is in play?

Just what did President Reagan mean when he signed the Free Trade Plus deal and said it was "a great day for civilization" and also "a new era of freedom"?

Just how is a rational person supposed to interpret Mulroney's speech to the UN in which he wrapped himself in the mantle of anti-poverty and pro-environment?

In this pre-dawn limbo on a Friday it's entertaining to speculate on all of the above.

If Ben Johnson confesses to knowingly taking anabolic steroids then for once the journalists are correct in using the term "tragedy". Tragedy as depicted by the ancient Greek dramatists involved a larger than life hero of almost superhuman accomplishments whose downfall came about as a result of a flaw in his own character, usually overweening pride.

The peculiar thing is that the dramatist's tragedy is supposed to have a cathartic effect upon the audience, purging us so violently of our emotions, through empathy for the hero, that we leave the theatre feeling cleansed.

I'm still waiting for the catharsis. This heartbreak I feel for Ben isn't purging anything. So much for the theories of drama.

But there's another if. What if Ben had steroids foisted upon him without his knowledge or consent? Ah, then it's not a classic tragedy but rather in the realm of high crime. Most certainly a crime of fraud — but also of assault, causing eventual bodily harm to Ben and spiritual harm to millions. On a lesser, national scale, such a crime verges on treason.

As for the Angus Reid poll, it does seem to indicate that the swine and slops theory is working. You may remember it as the theory of economics that equated the populace with swine having slops poured in front of them. The more slops the greater the contentment and the more practical the economics.

It seems too much of a coincidence for the Multory ratings to rocket upwards so abruptly in the wake of an unprecedented orgy of pre-election regional handouts. The prime minister is emptying the whole silo into the troughs and we are reacting in keeping with the theory. Fascinating.

In pondering President Reagan's optimism for both civilization and freedom I can't help but remember the economists who recently prophesied on CBC's Journal that the great trading blocs of the future will leave out most of South America and all of Africa. I must assume that the president has a rather narrow definition of civilization. We already know that he has a very limited interpretation of freedom. The rhetorical sophistry surrounding Free Trade Plus takes on new dimensions.

And if the said prophets are correct then our prime minister's UN pose as an environmentalist, and as one having concern over the widening gap between rich and poor nations, becomes truly paradoxical. The Free Trade Plus deal is designed to create one of the great blocs that will exclude poor nations and is intended to stimulate the industrial growth that is helping to destroy the global environment!

I find all this difficult to comprehend. But wait. An analogy strikes me. It brings together Olympic scandal, swine and slops, Free Trade, and all the rest. The comparison is that the Multories, in striving for economic gain and political longevity, are trying to put Canada on steroids.

The analogy is complete, including the implication of moral corruptness. And if we agree knowingly, it's a tragedy. If it's foisted upon us in our ignorance, it's a crime.

For Your Notes: